MAKING
THE MOST OF
LIVING
ROOMS

MAKING
THE MOST OF
LIVING
ROOMS

A M A N D A   E V A N S

RIZZOLI
NEW YORK

For Andrew

First published in the United States of America in 1998 by
RIZZOLI INTERNATIONAL PUBLICATIONS, INC.
300 Park Avenue South, New York, NY 10010

First published in Great Britain in 1998 by
Conran Octopus Limited
37 Shelton Street
London WC2H 9HN

ISBN 0-8478-2128-5
LC 98-65891

Commissioning Editor	Denny Hemming
Project Editor	Sarah Sears
Designer	Amanda Lerwill
Picture Research	Helen Fickling
Production	Julian Deeming
Illustrator	Sarah John

Printed in China

CONTENTS

INTRODUCTION

Modern domestic life is tending more and more towards the informal so that what was once the space set aside solely for formal entertaining is now frequently the hub of the house, where all manner of activities takes place.

Until relatively recently each room in the house had a particular purpose and that definition was pretty clear-cut. A drawing room was where you entertained formally; a dining room was where you ate; a library or study was where you worked – for business or pleasure. A nursery or playroom was the children's domain. Massive changes in social behaviour have taken place over the past twenty years or so, however – in entertaining, cooking, eating, work and leisure time, and in family life generally – so that many of us have turned our backs on such ingrained rules. The requirements we now have for what is called the living room are very much more ambiguous.

The term 'living room' means exactly that. It is the space where the whole family lives its life. Whatever its size, it will have to cope with a complex set of demands. So, whilst, on the one hand, it may well continue to be furnished with the ubiquitous three-piece suite, and it is still likely to be the room in which we want to entertain in

uncluttered surroundings, it has also become the after-work retreat, where we watch television, chat, listen to or play music, browse through books and newspapers, or work at the computer – a room for which children have their uses too.

Inevitably, then, as the roles of the living room multiply, and this space is increasingly seen as the central focus of the home, so an accompanying new trend in decorating emerges. Dividing walls are being knocked down to accommodate a much bigger 'living' space. Basements are being excavated to create vast kitchens with one end devoted to a comfortable seating arrangement. If not visible, a television is almost bound to be hidden somewhere – often a computer and music centre too – as modern leisure becomes daily more high-tech-oriented.

Whether you opt for one room or a huge all-encompassing space, the most important thing about your living room is that it should be created around the your personal needs and priorities, so that it automatically becomes part of your life: the comfortable place to which your family and friends are magnetically drawn. The true test of your design will be whether you spend a lot of time in your living room.

BASIC PRINCIPLES

Now that we are less bound by tradition in the interior design of our homes, planning a living room is rich with opportunity. However, a living room today is likely to have more than one role, and the whole process can seem somewhat bewildering. Whether you intend to knock down walls, or to stay within the confines of an existing room, you should plan meticulously from the outset. Ask yourself at the beginning what you really want – this is the key to creating a multi-purpose room that meets both your aesthetic and your various practical criteria.

YOUR NEEDS

There is no doubt that today's lives are lived at a faster pace than they were in the past. Technology, far from giving us more time, has simply made us feel that there is always more that we could – and should – undertake in a day. Where and how we relax, therefore, has taken on a new and more profound significance.

The majority of people live within the traditional framework of a conventional house layout: generally, there will be one room downstairs set aside for cooking and eating, another for sitting and relaxing and, for those with the luxury of space, a dining room often used only for formal entertaining. Historically, the hearth used to be the heart of the home for practical reasons; before central heating became '*de rigueur*', people would congregate around the fire for warmth, minimizing fuel consumption too, as lighting would then only be required in one room. Somehow, staring at flames is still primordially mesmeric.

If, however, we lead our lives very differently from previous generations, why should we be constrained by traditional notions of how a house should be arranged, what function a particular space might have, and how it should be furnished and decorated? You might want your living room to remain a more formal space for entertaining; you might want to integrate it into the kitchen, or you may need it to be a generously sized family room that will accommodate a variety of activities. Pausing for a moment to think honestly about what you really want out of your living room will mean the difference between a room that is rarely used and one that becomes a happy focus of your home for both family and friends. To create a living room

that, by virtue of the lives we lead, must work on many levels is certainly a design challenge. It is not impossible. Whatever your aims, you will be surprised how easily you can achieve them if you plan carefully from the start.

The first step, whether you are starting from scratch or developing an existing room, is to sit down and evaluate your lifestyle. Do you like a quiet space to read and relax? Is entertaining in elegant surroundings important to you? Do you have a family that congregates in the evening, and who all seem to be doing different things at once? Who is at home when? Do the needs of your very young children come first at the moment? Make a detailed checklist of the activities that will take place in this room and remember to include the ideas and opinions of other relevant members of the family, to ensure that this becomes a room that works for all of you. Will this room end up being a television room? Are there hobbies to consider? If you have

OPEN-PLAN RECIPES

A large multi-purpose room seems to meet both the practical and emotional requirements of a family living in the technological society. Families can relax without feeling squashed; children of varying ages can pursue different activities with minimal supervision; the cooking host does not have to feel isolated from guests; and guests do not have to perch in a tiny kitchen if they want to chat to their host.

Consider whether you prefer to relax with your friends over supper or lie among soft cushions; if you cook a lot, will you feel happier eating 'in the kitchen', or will you want to hide away the functional aspects of your life. Here (right) there are acres of space and the kitchen neatly lines one wall, barely intruding upon the sitting space. The simple dining table cleverly links service and entertainment areas, and the day bed underlines the room's flexibility. Its occupants are free to choose whether or not to participate in the life of the rest of the room. Only rugs define the zones.

Obviously, you do need space for this: ask a structural engineer which walls you might safely knock down, and remember to cost out the project comprehensively before you start work.

very young children, is it also necessary to accommodate their needs in the room? It is amazing how, as soon as you start to put your thoughts down on paper, you will start to feel very clear about exactly what you want. The answers you come up with will determine not only where in the house you should site your living room, but how you will furnish it as well. Even the simplest issue, such as who generally answers the phone, can lead to some surprising design decisions.

Remember that families grow up, evolve and move on; the storage units you built for toys may be less useful in a few years, when you will wish that you had designed them with shelves just that little bit deeper and higher in order to house the now-compulsory computer or television. It

goes without saying that whatever you hope to do with your living room, combining the many and complex requirements of rest, relaxation, entertaining and family life with your preferred design style will always be a challenge. It will also require discipline. Establish at the outset what you want for this room, because all the decisions you make early on will have a major influence on how the room is used. Then plan your furniture, fittings and decoration accordingly. Be resolute: do not be bullied into having the computer centre stage if you had really hoped this room would be for entertaining. Similarly, if talking and reading are your preferred forms of relaxation, there is nothing so disruptive as a television; it always tends to monopolize all other activities in the room. Moreover, if you have to wade

A CLASSICAL PROFILE

It is perhaps a luxury today to have a room specifcally for formal entertaining. If you do have the opportunity to design a room for social occasions, however, it is worth bearing in mind that formal need not imply stuffy. Indeed, here (left), the classical heads and zebra-striped fabric in an otherwise simple design give the room a nonchalantly witty air.

Remember that you will need space around furniture for guests to circulate during larger events, but that closer, intimate seating groups will encourage conversation between smaller numbers.

Aim to design your room around seating plans that can be rearranged, and you will give the room a multiplicity of uses. An upholstered stool – used either as extra seating or as a coffee table – forms the focus here, although the size of the sofa is emphatic.

A large window provides ample light during the day – muslin half-curtains guarding against any potentially intrusive glare – while the table lamp replicates the light source during the evening. A narrow consul table behind the sofa accommodates this, a pair of topiary trees and a picture. Different artefacts and flowers here would alter the tone of the entire room significantly.

■ 1 3

FAMILY AFFAIRS

Ensuring that you have abundant storage capacity is the key to incorporating the needs of a young family into your living room without having to abandon your own desires completely in a sea of toys and games. If they can be quickly and easily hidden when the children go to bed, you will find it easier to regain your equilibrium at the end of a tiring day.

A large armoire or a trunk of wood or wicker (right) will store heaps of games, jigsaws and books. With the lid closed, a trunk will even double as a table.

You do not have to sacrifice style, as this pristine white living room (opposite) testifies. Even if grown-up books and possessions reside on the upper shelves, children's possessions can be hidden behind closed doors. For your own sake, keep precious ornaments well out of reach; children have little regard for nostalgia and sentimental value.

Children are unconscious of the consequences of sticky fingers and spilled drinks, but washable loose covers and rugs – rather than close carpeting – will allow you to reinvent your room after the inevitable minor disasters.

It is also essential to think about safety: sharp-edged furniture and slippery floor surfaces can prove lethal.

through a mountain of toys or piles of newspapers each evening before you can flop in comfort onto the sofa, the whole point of the room is missed.

Professional help

Whatever you are planning, give yourself a budget and stick to it. Lucky indeed is the person who can redecorate and refurnish a room in one fell swoop, and there is nothing like a tight budget to concentrate the mind on priorities and where you must draw the line. If you are considering major building work – a considerable financial investment – it is often worth employing a reputable architect or designer. It might seem like an expensive extravagance, but making uninformed and inappropriate decisions on this scale is costly too; in the long run, looking to a professional may actually save you money, which you can then enjoy spending on the decorative elements of the room. Because his/her livelihood depends on a good reputation, a professional should have both the knowledge and the right contacts to ensure that the work is not only carried out to the highest standards but that money is not wasted on unnecessary mistakes. Always try to use someone who has been personally recommended, and make an effort to go and look at some of their previous work to reassure yourself – even photographs can be deceptive. You are much more likely to identify a worrying detail when you stand in front of the real thing and talk to someone who has lived with the work.

Before you embark on an expensive option, find out if any of your friends or neighbours have done the same thing. Take a look at what they have achieved and ask them to tell you honestly about any problems they encountered. Not only will you get some useful advice and design inspiration, but this is often a good way to discover what you do not want in your own room.

Even on a more basic level, if you are simply stuck for ideas on how best to use and decorate the room, calling in an interior designer to give you some inspiration can still be money well spent. You do not need to employ them to do anything more than give you a few pearls of wisdom about how best to arrange furniture, storage and lighting – you may be amazed at how it can set you on the right track.

Starting from scratch

Those fortunate enough to be starting with a bare canvas should consider at this point whether the appointed room is the space best suited to become the living room. This is when another range of lifestyle questions becomes relevant. Do you work from home, and if so, will you be using a computer or a drawing board or any other special equipment? Or will this be more of an evening room to retreat into after a long day in the office? Do you have space for the luxury of a playroom or will your children be the room's most frequent visitors – to watch television, play, do their homework? How do you like to entertain: as a family at lunchtime at the weekends, very informally

WORKING SPACES

The beauty of modern technology is that it is flexible, and that more compact models are being developed every day, so it is relatively easy to set up an office in the hub of a living room. Tidy workers can use a dining table as a desk (right), as long as everything can be put away at the end of the day. Here simple box-shelf units can be wheeled to the table when required and yet blend into the room's decorative scheme once back against the wall. A drawing board and desk lamp (opposite) may similarly be packed away, shifting the focus of the room to the comfort zone – the coffee table and sofa. Even a narrow wall space can become an office (right below). All you need is some shelves – one a little deeper for a laptop computer, with drawers underneath.

Working from home requires a lot of discipline so try to design a work space to be both comfortable and efficient to make the call to arms as attractive as possible. You must be able to set up and clear away quickly too or a convenience will become a chore. Your worktops must be at a comfortable height; your chair should support your back; you must have enough light, and your power supply and telephone wires should be sited so that you do not trip over the wires.

after work during the week, or elegantly, as an antidote to mundane everyday routines? Does your lifestyle change from season to season, so that you entertain more in the winter when the dull days are short, leaving the summer for yourself, or do you tend to snuggle up in the cold, becoming more sociable when warm, golden evenings are the perfect backdrop for unwinding at the end of the day, whether alone or amidst company?

Look carefully at your proposed living room: which way does it face; how big are the windows; is natural light is important to you, and if so, how best can you take advantage of every minute of it – and the view if there is one? Sunshine is lovely when it slants into a room, but when it creates a glare on a screen, or shines straight into your face while you are trying to talk to someone, it is intrusive. Northern light is the most even, and therefore the most attractive if you are artistically inclined. If, in your mind's eye, your ideal room exudes an atmosphere of cosy snugness, think about whether the room will feel too big with big windows, or whether curtains will create an effective balance, adding proportion by day and warmth by night. Pause to think about how to arrange the furniture in order to take best advantage of the room's direction. Look at your house as if with fresh eyes. Perhaps the particularly large room upstairs would work better, and suit the needs of your family more comprehensively, than the one you have allocated on the ground floor. You might have a conservatory that would allow you to create a sunny outdoor feel, particularly if you exploit the indoor heat to surround yourself with Mediterranean plants heavy with scented flowers. Perhaps you can knock down a wall to create one big room from two. Alternatively, many houses

have basement space which runs the length and breadth of the house, and even though it is expensive to dig down, this is an increasingly popular way to create a tailor-made living room. Many contemporary conversions create exciting shapes to work with; do not be put off by empty spaces. Nevertheless, if you are considering any of these building options, it is worth remembering that although comfort is paramount, a room that sits awkwardly with the original architecture – or indeed the general proportions of the house – will never be successful.

One big room combining kitchen, eating and living areas, and yet with enough floor space to allocate a zone to each function, is a perfect arrangement for those who enjoy and encourage easy entertaining and a relaxed way of life. Eating habits have evolved dramatically alongside

PLANNING CHECKLIST

Before embarking on any work at all – whether major construction or a minor redecorating job – remember to:

- Identify your priorities: ascertain whether the room will be public or private, used primarily during the day or at night. Will it be noisy and sociable or quiet and contemplative?

- Make a written list of the activities you intend for the room so that you can plan adequately for everything.

- Try to visualize all your potential future requirements, not just those that are obvious now, and remember to include these in your considerations.

- Get everyone to contribute their views or you are bound to forget what one member of the family considers vital.

- Analyse any patterns that emerge in your answers in order to prioritize what needs to be done first.

- Allocate your available funds carefully, taking a long-term view; it is wise to hold back a contingency fund.

- Keep in mind that it will probably be less expensive to seek professional advice initially than to try to salvage the situation after a costly mistake.

- Give yourself a budget and stick to it rigidly: the stress of overspending will taint your opinion of the finished room.

TV BUFF

Screens both big and small are playing an increasingly large role in modern life as an ever greater proportion of our leisure time is devoted to film, television and video. So it is almost inevitable that a television will feature in your plans; the question then becomes how high a priority it should be. The television in this living room is given centre stage, while one solitary yet elegant rocking chair has been carefully positioned to provide optimum viewing conditions. The overall look of the room has also been carefully considered, however. The monochromatic design scheme takes its lead from the inevitable black television casing. White-painted floorboards and white walls are the foil for the graphic quality of the black-framed black-and-white photographs, hard-edged fireplace and the dark window frames.

The whole emphasis of this room is on relaxed viewing. The rocking chair, despite its contemporary design, carries with it traditional notions of peace and quiet. Plain white muslin filters the light, softening the austere atmosphere, and prevents reflections on the television screen. The curvaceous line of the quirky standard lamp plays an important role, too, a playful touch in the calm.

many other lifestyle changes over recent times so that food preparation in advance is no longer deemed a necessity for 'proper' entertaining. In a room designed with this in mind, impromptu invitations to stay for supper and additions to numbers of mouths wanting to be fed need no longer cause undue disruption. Given how we all tend to gravitate towards the cook, this does at least ensure that rather than being on top of one another in a tiny kitchen, friends and family can spread out, while the cook still feels part of the proceedings. Moreoever, an arrangement like this allows you to get on with something even if you are having to oversee others – supervising homework, for instance.

Floor plans and templates

Once you have decided on the location of the room and the many functions it must accommodate, a scale floor plan is vital. It does not have to be formidably professional; even a quick sketch, marking out any fireplaces, alcoves, windows, doors, sockets, radiators and existing lighting will help. If you can play on paper before you have to make decisions, you will be able to experiment with all the elements you want to fit in without undue and wasted effort. You will also be able to identify what is still missing.

Neatness is not essential, but working to scale is more important. A scale of 1:50 is generally considered to work well. Use graph paper to draw out the plan of the room, and then make yourself templates of any furniture you know you will be using, so that you can move them around in different permutations until you find one you like. The seating arrangement is crucial to a living room's success, and there are several guidelines that are worth bearing in mind when you are working out your layout, for it is the way you group your sofas and chairs that will encourage the different activities you have in mind for the room.

SPACE TO VIEW

The sheen of an expansive wooden floor, combined with a warm colour scheme, gives this contemporary living space an inviting glow, although, with few objects and no unnecessary pieces of furniture, the room is pervaded by a calm serenity. Anything that could be deemed clutter, as well as the music centre and the television, lots of books and magazines, has been given a home in the custom-built shelving units that run the entire length and height of the room.

The traditional three-piece suite has today been pushed aside in favour of a wide range of more flexible seating possibilities. Indeed, chairs and sofas no longer need to originate from the same period; nor do they need to be covered in strictly matching fabric. Here, for instance, conventional armchairs have here been replaced by a pair of modern chaises longues. While these appear to have been positioned with elegant enter-taining in mind – either *a deux* or in conjunction with the sofa – they are perfectly placed to recline in comfort in front of the television discreetly disguised among the bookshelves.

A glass-panelled wall partitions off the dining room without losing any sense of spaciousness.

UNDER GLASS

Conservatories are too often deemed suitable for summer use alone. Given a chance, a conservatory can make a perfect year-round living room.

Surrounding yourself with views of the outside will give you an impression of air and space – particularly beneficial if you live and work in a town. You will catch whatever sun there is throughout the year and, as long as the windows are double-glazed and your heating system is efficient, winter in a conservatory should be quite comfortable. There is nothing to stop you from having a roaring fire there (see opposite); the flickering flames and candles will seem almost magical reflected in the glass.

Your conservatory can act as a transitional stage between house and garden, so you should design your garden with the year-round views from inside in mind and vice versa. Frustrated gardeners can grow exotic plants as decorative details in the quasi hothouse. Here (right) Gothic trellis wall panels strengthen the outdoor, garden illusion.

Wicker furniture works well all year round and rugs, added for warmth in winter, can be taken up in the summer. Roof blinds will shield both family and guests from summer's harsh glare.

Use your ground plan to help you make decisions about the way in which you are going to arrange the furniture. It will also make it easier to work out a fairly comprehensive plan for the positioning of lights, television, hi-fi, and thus to establish exactly where you require electric sockets, and how many. There can be nothing worse than finishing your decorating, only then to discover that you need more electrical points, or that you now think you might prefer to have wall sconces instead of table lamps. As a general rule of thumb you can never have enough sockets, but that is no reason to be haphazard about where they are put. If you know in advance where you are going to want them, you can ensure that your living room never has ugly and potentially dangerous trailing wires, and that the electrical items are positioned where you would like them and not where you are forced to put them. Now is the moment, too, if you are already involved in building work, to make the decision to install a dramatic lighting scheme, bearing in mind that insufficient light and activities, such as reading and sewing, are mutually exclusive.

Storage can make or break a living room. If it is carefully worked out to meet your needs, it will not only become an integral part of the room's design but will enhance your enjoyment of that room. Haphazard storage, or none at all, does quite the opposite. This is where you hope to spend time with your family, entertain friends, relax, chat, watch television and listen to music, and you simply will not be able to do any of these with any degree of enjoyment if you are always surrounded by teetering piles of papers and if the floor is covered with the accumulation of the day's fun and games. The nature of storage will depend largely on the activities you plan for your living room. It must tackle

LIFE AT THE TOP

Conventionally the living room is found on the ground floor or, occasionally, upstairs. But why not in your attic? A living room at this height, even in a city, is likely to offer views of sky and trees – much more enriching than pavement. This loft (right) has been converted very simply. Two Velux windows in the eaves and a run of French windows leading out to a little balcony let in plenty of light. The stained wooden floor has been highly polished, which helps to reflect the light back into the room.

Architect-designed conversions of sites that might appear unpromising or offputtingly big to the layman are, in fact, particularly exciting; they offer interesting shapes and spaces to the inspired flat-owner to play with. This converted warehouse (far right) is unusually spacious and tall, but such a vast area need not be daunting; indeed, you do not have to furnish it as one room. You can break it up, as here, with small groups of furniture drawn together around a rug or table. Inject a light, airy shell with strong accents: colourful rugs and textiles, and bright pictures. A spiral staircase is a useful device if you want to create a sense of division without blocking either the light or the view.

the difficult task of providing you with the most practical solution for putting objects away, combined with a decorative appeal that suits the room: if you want your sitting room to seem calm, perhaps even minimalist, then it is likely that you will not want the contents of an open shelving system cluttering up the view.

Decide whether you want fitted or unfitted storage. If you are planning to have purpose-built storage, you will need to measure the height and depth of the possessions you plan to put away, because although this seems a tedious exercise, it will allow you to maximize your available space. Make another checklist – of the things you will need to store. Consider things like sewing, games, jigsaws, electronic equipment, music centres, newspapers, drinks bottles, glasses and toys. Take note of how many CDs, books and videos you actually possess, and remember how your collections will expand with time. Remember, also, that books, music, photograph albums and clutter inevitably accumulate over the years, so always overestimate the amount of storage you think you require; you will grow into any unused shelves surprisingly fast.

Fitted units have the advantage of being custom-designed to suit your purposes, but remember they cannot go with you when you move house. If you spend a little time at this stage doing some research both in exclusive department stores and at some of the larger, out-of-town furniture warehouses, you may be able to create a storage system out of shop-bought units that suits your needs perfectly, and that not only moves house when you do, but can be moved from room to room as your needs change.

It is quite likely that today's living room will have to double up as something else. For the many of us who do not have the luxury of a separate study, it may well, for example, be the room from which you also work. If you intend to have part of your living room as a study, there are plenty of ways to disguise your office after-hours. The simplest is a screen across one corner of the room, behind which you can hide the whole thing – desk, computer and the mountains of paper that so often accumulate. You might consider building a neat, self-contained office unit out of a full-length recessed cupboard space. Fitted with plenty of shallow shelves for your computer and any files, papers and books you need, it could create several extra feet of office storage when open, and with double doors across the front, it can be hidden at the end of the day.

Office storage does not need to look utterly functional, it can look good too. Ottomans that hold files are a boon – and there is nothing so satisfying as sweeping a pile of papers into such a black hole and closing the lid as an unexpected guest turns up. These benches can be covered in fabrics to suit the style of your room, and have the added advantage of doubling as extra seating when required.

No matter what you want to do in your living room, it should still be a calm and peaceful place to which you can retreat. Good planning and careful thought at the early stages will ensure you achieve this.

ESSENTIAL FIRST STEPS

- View each of your rooms as a potential living room in order to choose the one best suited to your needs. Can you combine the living room with the kitchen, study, conservatory or playroom? Can you dig down, or convert the attic?
- Having identified your site, point out your room's good points as an estate agent would to a prospective buyer: note both the things you particularly like about the room, and features, like alcoves, which are more significant than they appear.

- Make an accurate groundplan on graph paper, with templates for your furniture, and use this as your master plan.
- Plan your furniture around a focal point – a mantelpiece, a painting or a piece of furniture. Remember to give yourself as much storage capacity as possible for everything issuing from all the activities likely to happen in your living room.
- Make a note of the fixtures that will require electrical sockets – lighting, hi-fi, television, computer and video. Ensure that you have enough sockets and position them sensibly.

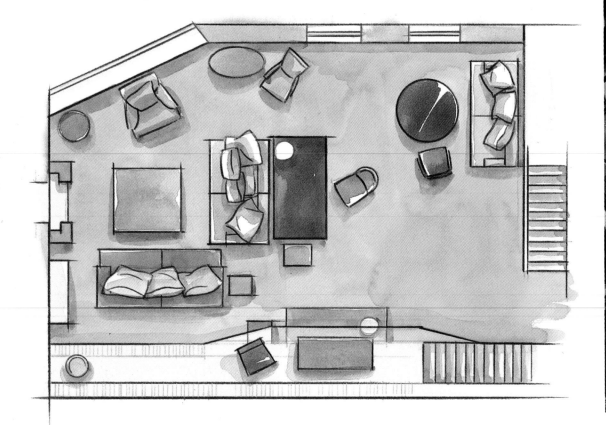

FAMILY PLAN

This is a perfect example of how distinct zones can be established successfully in a large space to create a truly multi-funtional family room. The furniture is arranged in small groups, each for a different purpose, whilst a sense of unity is retained in the room as a whole.

The area in front of the fire has been designated as a relaxation zone, with two sofas and an armchair grouped around the square table, which serves as both coffee table and extra seating. A table butted up to the back of the sofa becomes a separate writing/working space, a surface for ornaments and a table lamp for those seated on the sofa. The armchair, with its table beside it (top), can form another quiet seating area, or the chair can be drawn into the main group if required.

One whole wall (left) has been turned into a library, with desk and chairs on a gallery providing a chance to work away from the hub of the room.

Somewhat surprisingly for such a huge space, the decorative style is quite conventional, with patterned upholstery fabrics and heavy brocade curtains. The tree introduces a human scale, provides delicate textural variety and balances the height of the book-lined wall.

■ 25

EATING IN THE OPEN

Although often the envy of many people, large open spaces like this can be very awkward to furnish. All too often they end up looking barn-like, uninviting and intimidating instead of spacious and welcoming. The owners here have played subtly with vertical and horizontal lines to create a sense of division between living and dining areas without losing any advantage in the real dimensions of the long, airy room.

The level of the seating area has been raised with three steps (right above and below), which gives it its own distinct boundary. The chairs and sofa have been configured around a small square sisal rug and coffee table, which maintains an intimate feel even within the large room.

The dining 'room' at the bottom of the steps (opposite) is positioned closer to the kitchen for easy access; with glass on two sides opening onto a spectacular view of glittering water, the table stands alone, uncluttered by other furniture.

The warm wooden floorboards have been laid in different directions – along the length of the living area and across the dining area – to accentuate further the separate spaces and also to break up, with an interesting visual pattern, the vast expanse of floor.

FURNISHING AND FURNITURE

Once the location has been chosen and you have decided how your living room is going to be used, it is time to think about the sort of furniture, fixtures and fittings that will best achieve your aims. Making comfort a priority for your living space is neither as obvious nor as simple as it might appear. Comfort is complex and multi-layered; it involves efficiency, convenience and ease. The challenge now is to decide on furniture, lighting and storage that might be appropriate and then to arrange it effectively.

SHOCKING PINK

It may be tempting to choose diminutive furniture when you live in a small house with small rooms. This room (right) has made size its virtue, by positioning two large sofas, with generously heaped cushions, at right angles to each other. Equally, two sofas and an armchair would provide a very flexible alternative: the sofas could be positioned opposite each other or at right angles, and the armchair moved in or out of the group as required.

Two sofas facing each other or at right angles to each other, using a coffee table as the central focus, will allow for both intimate conversation and entertaining on a larger scale. It is an expansive gesture which makes the room seem bigger than it actually is. Two low, cushioned poufs make the seating arrangements even more flexible because they can double as side tables, or as extra seating when necessary.

The whole emphasis of this room is one of relaxed conversation and easy entertaining. Located in a traditional cottage, the room has been given a contemporary edge by the simple seating and the bold strength of colour. A single block of pink, highlighted by the bourgainvillea, is both bold and inviting. There is no need to clutter the small windows with fabric – the simple shutters do the job perfectly.

Seating

No matter what activities you plan for your living room, an arrangement of sofas and armchairs is likely to be the central focus; whether the room is immediately welcoming and comfortable will depend largely on the type of seating you choose, and way in which you group your furniture. The best arrangements will emerge when the functions of the room are considered alongside what looks best.

The type and the scale of your furniture will often be determined by the style, size and shape of your room, but what matters most is that you find furniture that suits its purpose. Do you need to accommodate numerous different functions in this one room? If so, it may need to be zoned to work well and skilful positioning of furniture can do this without losing any sense of the overall design scheme. If you plan to entertain, ask yourself what seating groups will make for the best conversation. Bear in mind that a group of people will instinctively form themselves into a loose circle as they chat.

Working around a focal point – a fireplace or a coffee table, for instance, is the most traditional option – make sure that your furniture is arranged to accommodate your guests comfortably into such a shape. Play around with different permutations on your plan using the templates of the pieces of furniture you intend to use. In a large room the sofas and chairs will need to be away from the walls, forming a self-contained group, or people will be shouting at each other across a chasm. Remember, though, to allow enough space in front of furniture for people to stand up and sit down easily. In a smaller room, furniture can be pushed against the walls. There is no point in having a neat little three-piece suite if you regularly have six people wanting to sit down at once, but too many chairs and sofas will turn your living room into a waiting room. Create arrangements that can be moved about easily.

Creating contrasts of shapes will add an extra visual dimension: a curved seat in a square room will soften any hard lines, while a long, thin room can be divided, and will appear wider, if L-shaped seating is used.

Investing in new furniture

Deciding to buy new furniture involves a major investment so do not skimp on research. Find sofas you like the look of, then sit on them, bounce on them, even put your socked feet up on them. It is the only way to be sure that the back will support you comfortably; that you can get in and out easily; that you know you will happy to chat, watch television or read from that sofa. Be completely objective about the furniture you already have; if something looks bulky or is dwarfed by the room, sell it and use the money to buy exactly the right piece. Equally, it might be better to swop your three-seater sofa for a neater version that seats two. The old adage, however, that you get what you pay

NATURAL CALM

This traditional-looking room (left) has undoubtedly been designed for chatting, entertaining and relaxing. No matter whether large groups or small, intimate numbers are involved, the adaptability of the seating caters for all possibilities. Opposite a commodious sofa, flanking the fireplace, comfortable armchairs sit under deep, commodious bookshelves. White linen covers throughout give this room its co-ordinated look. Natural fabrics dominate, which cumulatively add to an atmosphere of luxurious calm.

The window bay provides an extra seat. If you are lucky enough to have a window bay or an alcove, it could provide an important aspect of the room, for everyone, however gregarious, needs space for themselves: here is a perfect refuge, a place to go and read quietly, away from the hubbub. A chair that might not seem to fit your design plans, but which you know and love, might fulfil the same function.

Often overlooked at planning stage, a coffee table is also important because, as a visual and physical link, it will draw together a disparate collection of chairs and sofas to create a sense of order, and provide an important surface for game-playing, magazines, books and meals.

SITTING COMFORTABLY

The central focus of any living room is inevitably the seating; the sofa-to-chair ratio and the type of seating you choose will depend on what you want out of the room. Soft, low sofas are wonderful for reading or Sunday snoozing but they are not ideal for anyone who entertains a lot: talking from an inferior height can make guests feel self-conscious and they are likely to end up perching awkwardly. Meanwhile, whilst Gustavian-style wooden sofas make a chic statement, they are not good for family relaxation.

In an unusual arrangement (opposite) there is a low wooden bench where one might expect to see another sofa – ideal if flexibility is a priority, as the bench can be moved at a moment's notice. Bear in mind (above left) that a three-seater sofa is usually only used by two people at once, but always looks welcoming. A group of armchairs (above right) is a very flexible option, as they can easily be moved about when necessary, but take care that the effect does not feel too scattered. Aim to create a sense of unity through material or colour instead. Wicker (bottom left) is a refreshing option. This layout feels a little formal, yet the simplicity of colour scheme and design gives it a welcoming appeal.

BRIGHT LIGHTS

Even if natural light streams into your living room by day (opposite left), you will still need lights to perform a variety of different tasks; general overall light will probably need to be supplemented by task lighting. The downlighters here (right) have been incorporated into the design scheme, rather than being hidden in the ceiling. The metal shades, hanging low over the various objects underneath, have really become part of the display, as well as doing the job of highlighting the side table. The twin candlestick lamps will supply a gentler light, a subtle echo of its natural counterpart. Table lamps should be considered as an important decorative element, even when they are not switched on.

A smart, contemporary alternative to the traditional standard lamp, a low-voltage halogen lamp (opposite right) can be angled in any direction, making it the ideal reading lamp for anyone seated on the sofa. Wall-mounted swing-arm lights also give excellent reading light, can be dimmed to suit the occasion, and are very useful alternatives to table lamps. If your living room has to double as an office, a halogen lamp will look smart as well as providing the best concentrated light source for the desk.

for is generally true. It is worth spending what seem to be large sums of money on furniture, as a fully sprung sofa is more comfortable and will wear better than its cheaper foam counterpart. Consider it an investment in comfort.

Lighting

Good lighting relies on achieving a flexible quality of light that can change to suit the room's mood without compromising your practical needs. Here is your chance to create a sense of theatre.

Choosing the correct design of lamp is crucial too. Generally, living rooms rely on overhead lighting but there are some very sophisticated ceiling and wall lights available now – no longer clumsy, over-bright spots, but low-voltage halogen wall-washers, down- and up-lighters. Augmented by table lamps, which can be turned on and off in different permutations, these will create a sense of atmosphere to suit any occasion The much-disdained dimmer switch might also prove invaluable. Obviously, the more lamps you have, the more variations of mood at your disposal.

Plan your lighting as precisely as possible as early as possible; it should not be an afterthought. You will not want to pull down a newly decorated ceiling, so do not underestimate the problems that sophisticated lighting systems can create. Talk to a lighting consultant and visit a specialist showroom to look at the latest effects – before you embark on any building work.

Use either a new-generation recessed halogen spot or a traditional picture light to draw attention to a painting. To provide strong, directional light for leisure activities, use task lighting. Imagine where you might sprawl with a book, or where you will sew, and be sure you have enough light. Ensure that each lamp will have a socket nearby.

BANISH CLUTTER

Good storage is essential for your own sanity and the best storage scheme has always been carefully planned in advance to accommodate exactly what needs to be stowed away. Even day-to-day paraphernalia can pile up alarmingly. You can never over-estimate your storage needs; there will always be things that need to be stored. Make your storage list comprehensive – include everything from paperwork to china and glassware – so that you do not waste money on the wrong units.

Freestanding units can move house with you and can often suit the intrinsic character of a room better than built-in cupboards, so do not dismiss them for their lack of streamlining. An unusual combination of cupboard space and plan chest, this vast armoire (above right) would be ideal for an artistic family or in a home office – though too inflexible to be more generally useful.

Storage on open shelves becomes display. Repeated square shapes in this room (below right) establish an ordered feel, and while the thickness of the shelves might seem extravagant, this weight of line does transform what is essentially a boring shelf into an example of simple but stylish design.

Different light bulbs produce widely divergent qualities of light. Traditional tungsten-filament light bulbs produce a warm light. They are available in a range of intensities and also as reflector bulbs, which are good for downlighters, wall washers and task lighting. Undeniably expensive, low-voltage tungsten halogen bulbs will produce a brighter, sharper light, but they must be run off a transformer.

Storage

Having worked out exactly what you want to stow, it is time to decide which storage method best suits your purposes. Remember that it needs to reflect the design and character of your room: antique glass display cabinets will look quite out of place in a contemporary family setting. A room for entertaining will be a nightmare if toys, games and puzzles are always spilling from narrow shelves.

Of the freestanding units, modular storage systems comprising a series of basic matching shapes of compatible size and style allow you to mix cupboards and shelves in quantities that suit you, and also to expand as and when needed. A modular system can be bought quite inexpensively in the large furniture warehouses, and a chic paint finish in a smart colour can completely transform a basic flat-pack unit. Single freestanding pieces, such as bookcases, sideboards and cabinets, can sometimes suit the look of a room better than an entire wall of organized storage: you might find an antique piece, but there are also some very stylish contemporary sideboards. Be aware, however, that for the amount of space these items occupy, there is less actual storage volume. Simple ottomans and wooden trunks can be more hardworking: they are the perfect place to put away all manner of odds and ends, and

OPEN VERSUS CLOSED

While an antique cabinet might enhance your living room's appearance, it may not be flexible enough to cater for your more modern requirements. Custom-built storage, on the other hand, can actively and precisely exploit every available inch of space in alcoves and awkward areas that might otherwise be wasted. Several differently sized cupboard spaces are here (left) hidden behind a series of doors, all painted the same colour to retain a sense of unity, but given a faint sculptural quality by the irregularly positioned simple handles.

Much relaxation today is based on high-tech equipment, so siting electrical sockets and hiding wires will be very important. If you choose to house your hi-fi and its components, a custom-built unit could be made to measure. The machine will be dust-free, but easily accessible (you do not want to have to crouch or climb a ladder whenever you want music) and you will be able to hide away both the requisite number of power points and what might otherwise become a mess of trailing wires and extension leads. Think about where your speakers should stand, too, in order to make the most of the room's acoustics; perhaps these should also be hidden.

can be used as extra seating or as a table. Even piles of old newspapers will instantly look neater stacked in baskets or trays on just such a freestanding shelf.

While freestanding items can be moved around easily from room to room – even house to house – built-in storage, by its very nature, will be more an intrinsic part of the room's decorative design. If you have planned well, it should also suit your needs better than anything shop-bought. You should view more expensive custom-built furniture as a long-term investment. It can range from simple bracketed shelving to elaborate combinations of shelves and cupboards, even a window seat in a bay window – to be used either as low-level concealed shelving or, boxed in with the seat hinged as a lid, as a trunk. You cannot move built-in furniture, so work out how much display and how much hidden storage you need before you start work. If there is a gap between the tops of the books and the next shelf, you will have wasted space; and if a box sticks out of the cupboard, it will irritate you constantly. Calculating the proportions of the space you require is time well spent: look at your checklist of things needing to be stored, group them sensibly, and use the largest and smallest dimensions. If your budget is tight, why not hide adjustable shop-bought shelving behind custom-built doors? Open shelving is always extremely versatile. Storage is transformed into display on open shelving, and new contents will transform a room's look dramatically. Decide which things should go on display and which would be better behind closed doors.

Accessibility must be the key, so establish which things you need on a regular basis and at what height; games only played once a year should stay at the back of a cupboard.

SIGHT UNSEEN

Few televisions are attractive enough to put on display; indeed they are quite intrusive when visible all the time. Purpose-built storage units are all too often even uglier than the television itself, and they are less than likely to suit your decorating style. It is relatively easy to customize a piece of furniture yourself in order to hide the ugly grey box, or a music centre, behind a more decorative façade of a cabinet. This painted pine cupboard (left), originally the bottom of a dresser, serves the purpose perfectly, sits very well in this simple white room, and effectively provides an ideal display surface for a selection of vases and boxes (opposite above). Its bulk is balanced by the wooden trunk across the room, which offers more storage and display potential for boxes and books.

It is not difficult to transform storage into attractive display. Boxes of varying capacities can be (opposite below) stacked emphatically high on a table, their soft cream toning with the room's pale colouring. While they may contain all manner of chaos, this fact is so well disguised that, in effect, disorder is made an important and integral part of a very ordered design statement.

STYLE

It is an instinctive, emotional response to certain atmospheres that creates style – the unique element in decorating that inevitably evolves out of your own personality. Thus, whilst you may use photographs and books for inspiration, the way you reinvent a certain look in your own living room will depend utterly on you. Style transcends fashion and period distinctions; there are no rules you must obey as you develop your own particular style. You must simply trust your instincts and the rest will follow.

PLAIN AND SIMPLE

Nature is effortlessly elegant, so a room that is designed around organic colours and materials tends to exude a feeling of calm and unfussy stylishness: as they do in the wild, the colours of nature tend to tone, sitting happily next to each other. Moreover, natural textures seem to age gracefully too, like fruit ripening in the sun. Nothing in this living room (left), designed exclusively with natural ingredients, seems to jar: disparate shapes and ideas, periods and styles have been combined successfully in a cool but welcoming interior that has a timeless, classic quality. The round table and armchair might, covered in a floral fabric, have looked very traditional, but in plain white, and alongside the dark leather sofas and tôle butler's tray, they create the sort of textural contrast which gives this room its modern appeal.

The sense of uncluttered simplicity is emphasized by the wide floorboards and by the lack of curtains – no flowing lines of draped fabric to distract the eye from the clean lines of the interior.

In a similar vein, a cotton bolster and ticking cushions lend a modern angle – and a degree of comfort – to the antique wooden settle (right) standing beneath a pair of walnut-framed marine prints.

GRASS ROOTS

Taking natural materials as the basis for a decorating scheme is nothing new. What is extraordinary about these ingredients is that they seem to be timeless. In America they were used by the Shakers well over two hundred years ago to create elegantly functional interiors. And much country style is still built around different combinations of such simple elements. Yet the artful simplicity that results from mixing such ingredients also produces strong, crisp lines that work perfectly in today's modern home. Indeed, the term 'natural' immediately conjures up an image with a strong, contemporary twist, far from a nostalgic country look. It is not even necessary to furnish the room with contemporary furniture; the dramatically effects created by mixing leather with linen, stone with muslin, wood with metal, will create a contemporary chic.

Any colour that you select for walls and woodwork in such a scheme will inevitably be taken from a natural palette. This does not mean, however, that you will be restricted to a monochromatic look. Paint ranges become ever more sophisticated, and historically accurate colours are now being revived, so the number of suitable tones is constantly growing. Think of the materials you plan to use and translate them into colour – sludge, putty, clotted cream, soft greys, slate blue are but a few. Glossy white woodwork is too harsh here; try using a matt finish instead. A soft stone or lichen colour will become an integral part of the natural scheme without dominating the room.

Aim to create strong contrasts to give this look a contemporary edge. One bold element that sets off the rest of the colour scheme will enliven it and give it strength.

For instance, you should make a virtue out of one piece of dark furniture. Give it space. And surround it with lighter colours and materials so that it can make a statement. Do not feel obliged to disguise a mantelpiece that does not quite go with the scheme. It will give you the chance to incorporate other interesting textures into the room.

Flagstones, bricks, or terracotta tiles are the obvious answer on the floor for a clean-lined natural look, but on a practical level they might be considered too cold an option for a cool climate. Wood always appears warm, so if you discover floorboards that are in good condition, they could be sanded and either matt-varnished or finished with a colour wash. Alternatively, if you prefer to have some sort of carpet, any of the huge range of natural floor-coverings now available will add both warmth and textural interest.

A DELFT TOUCH

The strength of this Long Island living room is derived from a clean, self-confident use of fresh blue and white. The shell of the room is painted white – walls, floorboards, coffered ceiling and window frames – and the white plates on the white coffee table build on these monochrome foundations. The table made out of clothes pegs is topped by a delicately white vase too.

The loose covers for the ample, traditionally shaped armchairs and sofa juxtapose stripes and flowers in various shades and intensities of blue, while the collection of serving platters and dinner plates on the wall takes up the theme, their haphazard arrangement adding to the room's relaxed air.

Warmth underfoot is offered by the flatweave rug on the floor, which also provides the seating arrangement with a sense of demarcation, both physically and visually, as the blue lines draw together the blues of the sofa and chairs.

Nature often provides the perfect textural detailing. Groups of pale sea pinks in galvanized metal tins (far right) can achieve visual strength in numbers, with stones from the beach completing the simple little still-life inspired by and indeed collected from the seaside.

FRESH BLUES

Blue has been combined decoratively with white for many centuries. It has been a perennial favourite in a wide variety of media, decorating porcelain in the East, ceramics and china and fabric across Europe; even today period French toile de Jouy prints are constantly reinvented in response to a continuing demand for classic but subtle patterned fabric. The fact is that blue and white is a timeless alliance, one that works as well in a slick city apartment as in a faded beach hut, in a contemporary setting or a home imbued with nostalgia. Even when the tones are faded, there is a freshness that is always appealing.

Today this two-colour combination is probably most often associated with the comfortably bleached look reminiscent of East Coast seaside homes and beach huts, lazy, hot sailing holidays and children in straw hats. But you do not have to live anywhere near a coast to create this sense of open space, pale airy colour and calm peace.

You can reproduce the look really very simply. No matter how eclectic your mix of furniture, or how many different patterns you use, they will be pulled together into a co-hesive style if you use blue and white as the dominant motif. Avoid choosing the same blue throughout as this will create too co-ordinated a look; search out a whole range instead, and be confident about combining different patterns – mixing fabrics can be fun. Like this you can marry antiques with contemporary objects; faded flowery chintz with crisp stripes; country china with stark metal.

The walls and floor are important ingredients. Indeed, for an authentic beach-hut look, you may even want to line the walls entirely in tongue-and-groove cladding. Less

expensively, simply choose the palest of paint colours – soft white or a gentle lavender blue, perhaps – to create an unobtrusive, airy shell. It might not be practical to keep the floorboards bare in colder climates. If you paint them white and lay a rug in the middle of the room where there will be the most traffic, you can still enjoy their casual style.

Intensify the look with bold collections of blue-and-white objects; no matter how disparate in shape, displayed together they will assume a strong unity. Look to nature, too, and you will find that the simplest natural things can be placed together with dramatic results: smooth stones and pebbles, wispy grasses, simple plants and gnarled pieces of driftwood all carry overtones of a windswept beach, and all display layers of texture and tone.

PALE JEWELS

Traditionally this elegantly scruffy decorating style has been epitomized best in English country houses and is born, genuinely, of generations of wear and tear and – more and more – of a lack of funds to redecorate. However, with the right ingredients, you can recreate something of the faded pallor of this look without having to wait for years for it to evolve: a bit of sanded-down woodwork here; some faded velvet throws there; a tapestry; a battered armchair; and a carefully distressed paint finish on the walls.

While perhaps its essence does not come naturally to the contemporary at heart, this look has grown increasingly popular among those who want a traditional feel without being overpowered by the trappings of chintz and flowers. It works best in rooms with a sense of the scale of grand architecture – though the room itself might be tiny – and requires you to trawl antique shops and flea markets for heavy velvet curtains, bergère chairs and sofas well worn with use. You should concentrate on the correct individual elements, rather than on a self-consciously polished finish; every ingredient has to work in its own right, however humble. You will, however, be able to juxtapose furniture and fabrics that might look odd anywhere else; indeed, you should layer rich fabrics and glorious weavings one upon the other. While this might look gaudy and overdone if they were brand new, here the effect is one of opulence. A fineness of form is essential throughout.

Twentieth-century technology does not sit well here; the room seems to yearn instead for conversation pieces, candlelight and entertaining, feeling empty without people and without whole logs burning in the fireplace.

SIESTA HEAT

The recent massive growth in foreign travel and the increased accessibility of far-flung parts of the world means that we are now receptive to a broader range of influences than ever before. Global style has evolved in response to our fascination with the art and design of these other cultures; it is about the marriage of contemporary living with tribal craft traditions from around the world. Thus, you should not feel the need to sacrifice the practicalities and luxuries of modern living in order to accommodate this style in your home. Indeed, at its best, a global look will have a timeless quality that will enhance any home.

Do not be tempted to design a room based entirely on happy memories of a single holiday: without the correct climate, architectural style and mood, which all have a significant bearing in creating an atmosphere, you will undoubtedly be disappointed. A little goes a long way, however, and if you have just one or two original pieces as the core of your design – a bright rug, perhaps, or a striking wooden bench, or a display of roughly thrown cooking pots on a table – you can then add a backdrop of deep, chalky colour to capture the mood and complete the look: choose terracotta, burnt umber, ochre, or deep yellow. You might even consider rubbed-back plaster on the walls.

Global style is associated with the cool, shaded look reminiscent of interiors in a hot climate, from a subtropical setting drenched entirely in colour to an airy, whitewashed Mediterranean room highlighted by details in bright azure and terracotta. It is characterized by warmth and colour, the intensely rich hues of dark woods and the natural dyes used to colour everything from ceramics to textiles.

QUIET CALM

The basis of any Oriental scheme is about maximizing the harmony in your living environment by following ancient rules relating to the flow of energy – known as *chi*. At its best this can positively promote feelings of peace, serene calm and uncluttered relaxation. However, a substantial degree of discipline is required to make this style work; an echo of the monastic austerity at the root of this tradition needs to be brought into play. The inhabitants of a room designed to recreate this atmosphere must be able to derive comfort – both physical and emotional – from stark simplicity; this is definitely not for sentimentalists.

It is perhaps no surprise amid the increasing stresses of everyday life today, that feng shui, the Chinese art of living in harmony with your environment, is becoming more and more popular in the West. The way to achieve this harmony

involves orchestrating to best advantage the relationships and natural rhythms of the different energies that affect us daily: the interaction of the complementary yin and yang of Chinese philosophy, a dynamic which works with opposites – light and dark, soft and hard, smooth and rough.

A meditative space is uncompromising, so if your inner spirit feels ill at ease with this look, it is a mistake to embark on creating one just for fashion's sake. You are unlikely to derive any feeling of safe haven or welcome from your room, and you will not want to spend any time there – a waste of effort, however beautiful the finished design.

If, on the contrary, the look appeals both aesthetically and emotionally, it is worth reading around the subject before you begin to acquaint yourself with the basic principles: why soft curves and rounded corners have a positive effect on the flow of energy, for example, while angles are more disruptive in nature, causing confusion. Do not, however, feel that you have to adhere slavishly to the rules. It is important that the fundamental construction of the room – the look and shape of walls, windows, ceiling – should be in keeping with the pared-down, linear look, but you should trust your senses and allow your own inner spirituality to get involved when you furnish and decorate the space. Although the curtains, cushions and invitingly soft sofas usually associated with welcoming warmth may be lacking, scrupulous attention paid to certain structural aspects of the room – underfloor heating, well-sealed windows and effective, unobtrusive lighting – will ensure that comfort will still play an essential role.

Commitment is vital. There can be nothing material, no clutter to disturb your spiritual quest; this look is about eliminating exterior distractions to liberate your inner self.

REFLECTIVE SPACE

The sparse distribution of objects in this room gives an initial impression of geometric precision. It becomes obvious on closer inspection, however, that what is of the utmost importance is a feeling of balance. For all the hard edges, there are organic forms and naturally flowing curves; potentially oppressive shades of black and grey are lifted by splashes of rich orange, with leafy greens beyond. Bright sunlight is counterpoised by a range of mellow shades, and a sense of equilibrium is created that is central to Oriental principles of harmony.

This look requires both discipline and commitment but it does not forego wit. Even the bench, apparently a heavy, horizontal black rectangular mass, is soft and welcoming, and it seems almost to float, so fine are its metal legs. The lone chair's unusual lines belie its ergonomic efficiency; it is very comfortable too.

In a more traditional home such an expanse of glass and streaming sunlight is unlikely, but it would be possible to recreate something of this sensation of calm spaciousness. Combine perfect circles with straight edges, and use reflective surfaces – be they mirrors, flat metal or highly polished furniture – to exploit what light you do have.

DECORATION

Decoration is a language; through it we are able to express our personal taste and create an overall ambience. The core ingredients of this language – colour, pattern and texture – are the mainstays of any interior design scheme. They are the key to assembling your living room's style so that it works successfully on many different levels. It does not matter so much how, or where, you use these ingredients; it is the way in which you interweave them that will allow you to create an individual room.

CREME DE LA CREME

Monochromatic schemes can have surprising diversity, for every colour has its own spectrum of tones, and will react in different ways to varying levels of light and reflection. Conversely, an eclectic range of design elements within one room can be united through the uniform use of a single colour. Here, a single-minded use of cream creates a successful marriage between antiques and contemporary objects and textiles. The lustre of mother-of-pearl buttons, opalescent glass and gleaming marble bring a feeling of baroque luxury to what is essentially a simple monochrome scheme. Metallic highlights add to this self-conscious but gleaming confection of like-coloured objects and textiles, assembled to show how tonal layering creates richness and depth.

Whilst cream is universally relaxing, other colours such as red and blue have a more idiosyncratic appeal and can affect different people in different ways. You can layer with tones of any colour that makes you feel comfortable, because the simplicity of such a scheme is easy on the eye. Instead of spending hours in pursuit of diverse colours that work together, why not decide to use your favourite colour and bask in it?

Decorating is about enhancing what you have. In the interests of economy, therefore, it is worth living in your room for a while before making any major decisions, for although decorating should let you feel creatively liberated, a degree of restraint may ultimately be more appropriate. The living room is in the public domain so your choice of colours, patterns and textures is particularly significant.

Colour

Colour can work magic. If you choose one that reflects your personality, you will create a room that relaxes you and makes your guests feel at home – no matter which end of the spectrum it comes from – because colour not only

CONTRASTS

Colours work on our emotions; they can make us feel happy, serene, energized, warm or animated – sad too, sometimes. Knowing this can make selecting a colour scheme for your living room really quite bewildering. Once you have established what you want from your room, however, and the mood or atmosphere you want to create, using certain colours will help produce that effect. Pale, neutral tones will evoke a relaxing atmosphere; bright contrasting colours create a stimulating room. An intimate, cosy effect is rooted in the warm end of the spectrum.

Stark white walls are the perfect foil for primary drama (above left). Strong colour is easy to live with, provided it is put together in simple blocks. The bright blues of the painting are well balanced by the boldly colourful furniture.

Although accents of colour have again been applied in a neutral shell (left), these bright colours work with each other, alongside the warm tones of cream walls and natural wood floor and furniture, to create a warm, relaxing effect. Citrus orange and green might, in theory, seem an unpromising choice for a tranquil room, but tones based less in hard lemon yellow than in red have been chosen here – and used with subtlety.

ROUGH AND SMOOTH

Do not underestimate the simple textural qualities of different fabrics, be they man-made or natural; they offer you enormous scope to select just the right look and feel for your room.

There is nothing like the inviting pile of velvet to add a touch of opulence. A light-absorbing material, velvet will make any colour look deeper and more luxurious. Distressed paintwork carries with it implied notions of age and supplies visual and tactile textural interest that tends to 'soften' a look. The contrast (above right) between the rich red velvet of the chair and its cushion, and the green wooden screen, is the key to the whole scheme's success. To juxtapose two such different textures, particularly in complementary colours, accentuates the qualities of each.

Light seems to dance on this still-life of self-patterned damask cushions (below right), creating a textural interplay that is just as interesting within a restrained cream-and-white colour combination. By adding a variety of decorative trims – from bobbles and tassels to fan-edged braids – you could give a dramatic edge to what would otherwise be an intensely subtle monochromatic statement in texture.

pulls a design scheme together on a visual level, it affects us emotionally too. The emotional effect of a colour alters from one environment to the next, so the direction your room faces and whether it benefits from lots of natural light will become important factors. Be wary of trying to recreate a colour scheme with nostalgic associations; it may not have the same emotional effect in a new environment.

Our perceptions of size, temperature and space can also be altered by colour. With the right colours, a dark room can appear lighter, a small room larger, a cold room warmer and a simple room grander.

Texture

Contrasts of texture are vital in most colour schemes, supplying an extra dimension or a dramatic visual accent. Texture can lift an otherwise rather flat scheme by playing with light; the constantly changing interaction of light and shadow on a variety of surfaces will always add interest.

Introducing texture into a room is easy. Here, just as in fashion, it is all about layers. The textural qualities of warm beech, rough hand-woven natural textiles or cool zinc are obvious. However, in order to create decorative schemes that combine textures successfully, it will be useful to understand how different textures behave.

Light-reflecting textures such as shiny gloss and vinyl silk emulsion paint, mirror, glass and metals all tend to bounce light back at you so the colour on such surfaces will look stronger and brighter, possibly even lighter. On the other hand, light-absorbing textures – matt paint, rich velvet pile, linens, cottons and wool, will make a colour look richer, dark and more subtle because the surface tends to swallow and absorb the light, and reduce the impact of

FEELING TACTILE

Texture will always add interest and an extra dimension to a colour scheme, so it is a vital consideration when you are decorating. You can make a small room seem more spacious and elegant by using light, cool colours, but this tiny flat also relies heavily on a range of textures to establish different levels of light and shade in the overall scheme.

Contrasts abound. Sliding doors with warm wooden frames and cool, frosted-glass panels separate the living room from the bedroom. A roughly hewn bowl from India sits on a smoothly grained cube table. The severe cold of the metal clothes locker stands in direct contrast to the soft velvet upholstery of the day bed. Even the shapes of the objects and lamps have tactile overtones, from the toothy outline on top of the clothes locker to the curvaceous, smooth shape of the lamp in the foreground.

Light – both natural and artificial – pours on to all these textures, and it bounces, is reflected and absorbed to a greater or lesser degree. With every tiny variation, each precisely positioned piece of furniture and each carefully selected ornament will take on new characteristics, but the room's tactile attraction will remain constant.

PLENTY OF PATTERN

Although we tend, when we talk about pattern in decorating, to think of fabrics and wallpapers, it can come from many different sources. In this simple white shell (right), pattern explodes from flat fabrics and three-dimensional displays.

Rooms that benefit from plenty of natural light are better decorated in airy, fresh colours – pale greens, yellows and blues. The overall design of this room is held together by its simple green-and-white colour scheme. The covers of the main pieces of furniture are plain, so the various green patterns on the cushion covers are given more emphasis: checks mix with fern leaves and crewel work, creating a lively effect.

Elsewhere in the room, the plain walls set off displays of objects that become patterns in their own right. Nothing could be simpler, for instance, than a row of fir cones along the top of a window. Their shapes and colours – even the gaps – give these curtainless windows a feeling of definition. Framed botanical paintings on the walls echo the paired panes of the windows and form a pattern in their own right. A plant theme links these with patterns around the room to unify the whole scheme: the leafy motif of the sofa cushion and the fir cones.

colour. Pierced screens, slatted blinds and shutters, cane and wicker, lace, diaphanous silks and sheer fabrics are all light-filtering, which will tend to give any colour scheme or design a greater sense of delicacy.

One or two strategically placed items – a metal-topped consul table, for instance, or a glass-topped coffee table, even a simply draped linen throw over a chair or sofa – can act as textural highlights in a more muted environment.

Carpet will soften any scheme. Equally sympathetic in traditional or contemporary schemes, natural sisal or coir matting is very popular but somewhat coarse; conventional carpet manufacturers are, however, producing very good imitations that create the effect without the roughness.

Pattern

In the nineteenth century interior design tended to be characterized by abundant, exuberantly strong patterns. Such a level of visual distraction would be intolerable today, and plain colour might seem more appropriate. You can, however, use pattern to break up solid colour and create different levels of interest, for a well-balanced pattern can mediate between strong shapes and plain colours to create the unity required in a well-organized space.

Most of us would probably immediately equate pattern with fabric, but paint effects and wallpaper are exciting areas to explore too. Moreover, pattern does not need to be two-dimensional: a strong display of cut glass, say, in a simply painted room would give as potent a sense of pattern as would a band of contrasting fabric on a curtain. Nor does it need to be a constant: the changing linear patterns created by natural light through Venetian blinds or slatted chair backs can provide stunning incidental details.

GREEN PEACE

Working with one single solid colour in a decorating scheme can be difficult to handle. Do not be fooled into painting a dark room in light colours in an attempt to make it seem lighter. It will merely look lacklustre and dull. Counteract the dark aspect with a colour from the other end of the spectrum instead; use warm shades of red or green and suffuse the room with a feeling of warmth.

Be aware that different materials will react to the same colour in dramatically different ways, so it is still possible to end up with a room that looks more like a complicated mess than a co-ordinated scheme. Use pattern – and texture – to break up solid colour and give it greater depth and interest.

The single-minded use of green here (left) is effective because of the varied patterns that work with, not against, each other. The tiny amount of white introduced in the patterns serves to lift the complexion of the room.

The plaid wallpaper, the spotty curtains, the multi-striped window cushion, the checked cushion and broad striped rug co-exist happily within the same bold colour palette. Yet each pattern is able to stand out individually and make its own statement.

You can use just one strong pattern, perhaps an animal print on one chair in the midst of a neutral colour scheme. Even a subtly self-patterned damask will 'lift' a room where uninterrupted colour might be too harsh on the eye. Alternatively, you can be bold, juxtaposing checks, stripes and floral prints on sofas and chairs, cushions and curtains, though it might be better in this case to use the same basic palette throughout to tie the scheme together.

PAPER AND WOOD

**What you put on your walls will define
the shape and style of your living room.
Classically striped wallpaper sets the
scene in this formal living room (right).
The combination of light and dark pinks
is easy to live with, and the vertical line
is picked up in the mantelpiece moulding
and again on the armchair's ticking.**

**Wood has long been a favourite wall
covering, usually in the form of panels or
tongue-and-groove cladding. It is seen
in its simplest form here (opposite), as
basic wooden planks painted white, the
lines echoing the floorboards. The use
of white wood as an all-encompassing
surface gives this room an airy, relaxed
feel – almost like a beach hut. Wood
introduces interesting textures into a
room that cannot be found in man-made
materials, and even varying the width
of the planks will have a surprisingly
dramatic effect on the style of the room.**

**One of the earliest ways of decorating
walls was to use fabric, and it can still
add a sense of warmth and texture that
is not possible to achieve with other
finishes. It will add a level of insulation,
too. Fabric is not easy to clean on walls,
however, so it would not be suitable in a
room doubling as a dining room – or in
a room used by children.**

Remember that the effect of a large pattern will be wasted on a small chair, or at a little window, and that small patterns will look insignificant at a big window or on large expanses of wall. A small swatch will be misleading so always ask for at least two pattern repeats in order to be able to judge more accurately the effect it will have *in situ*.

Walls

When you are planning your decoration you must think of the relationships that will emerge between the various elements rather than looking at each aspect in isolation. Thus, you should consider the walls of your living room in relation to the other surfaces; but be aware that what you do with your walls will tend to set the scene for the room. You may want the walls to play the leading role in your design but you may prefer them to act merely as a calm background for the design ideas within. Meanwhile, the state of your walls may have a significant bearing on what might at first seem a simple aesthetic decision; wood panelling can be used to disguise all manner of evils but will preclude the use of a floral wallpaper, for instance.

If you feel that paint is the answer, remember, when you are trying to decide on a shade, that colours always look stronger in quantity. It is almost impossible to choose from a paint swatch because your small sample will bear little resemblance to the finished effect. Paint sheets of paper instead – in the colours you are considering – and pin them up to give yourself a better idea of how the colours will look. As a general rule, opt for a lighter shade of your desired colour to get closer to the result you expected. Remember that paint can be mixed to match anything today, so if you have chosen a fabric, take a swatch of it

when you look for paint. If it is a patterned fabric, picking up on one of the detail colours rather than the background will create a more interesting scheme.

If you want to introduce a degree of texture, it is worth looking into paint finishes. Done by hand, they are less rigorously uniform than wallpaper patterns and, because they often require more than one colour – or even a range

COLOUR KNOW-HOW

Painting walls, woodwork, furniture – even floors – will be the boldest and quickest way to put colour into a room. The variety of shades available today is huge: from zingy modern ranges to more muted, historical authentic tones. You can find warm blues, lively greens and a hundred different whites.

Before you start to decorate it is very useful to know a little about a colour's character so that you understand what effect it will have on a room; a very eccentric scheme might put your guests on edge rather than allowing them to relax. Remember that the effect of colour changes with its intensity.

Red is the colour of aggression and energy. It can make you feel warm, so it is effective in cold rooms and good if you want to create a cosy atmosphere.

Orange is stimulating too. Use it in areas where you do not intend to relax.

Yellow is linked with sunshine, the intellect, creative energy and power. Use bright yellow to lift gloomy rooms, but with care – it is highly energizing.

Green is good for sunless rooms; it is refreshing and creates a feeling of space.

Blue is the colour of harmony and peace. True blue can seem cold, so warm it up with contrasting colours.

IDEAS FOR FLOORS

Floors should be considered on two levels; a strong design element in any room, they also serve a practical purpose. You should work systematically through all the practical advantages and disadvantages of the various options at the planning stage, bearing in mind the main functions and most frequent inhabitants of the room.

Stone or brick floors (above far left) are durable, stylish and easy to keep clean, but are cold under foot and a little less welcoming in appearance than close carpeting or rugs on wood. There is a huge and varied range of imported bricks and tiles now available and you can lay them in interesting patterns to elevate a room out of the ordinary.

Wooden floors (above left) have a look of pared-down simplicity that is perfect in a contemporary interior. Sanded down and painted, they form the perfect backdrop for any colour scheme or style. Scatter a few rugs for warmth underfoot. If you opt for wall-to-wall carpet (below left), try matching it with your wall colour for a stunning result.

The gleaming expanse of polished concrete in this converted warehouse (right) has an industrial edge that is entirely in keeping with the architecture.

of shades of a single colour – they can add a feeling of depth to a very simple design. The simpler finishes, like colour washing or combing, are easily mastered, but if you prefer a gesso or lacquer finish, you may decide to call in an expert to carry out the complicated work professionally. This is too important a room to get it wrong.

Before you make your final decision, remember to look at the room under all the lighting conditions that will exist there. It is quite startling how, even from early morning to midday, and certainly in natural daylight and in artificial light, colours and patterns can appear to change.

Floors

Floors can be left bare or covered in a wide variety of materials – simple wood, natural coir, stylish linoleum with a woven rug, even leather. The most conventional floor-covering is carpet – plain or patterned. Many traditional carpet-makers are adding wonderful new colours to their ranges, but be aware that dark colours, though better for muddy footprints, show more fluff than paler shades.

If you discover a wooden floor in good condition, why not sand it down and varnish it. Scattered with a rug or two, it will look very contemporary. Alternatively, you could

different shapes and sizes to define particular zones – around the fireside, for instance, tying sofas and chairs together to promote a cosy conversation area.

Natural floor-coverings such as jute or sisal are visually appealing but can be less than welcoming for bare feet. They are probably not the best choice if you have children – or friends who like to sit around on the floor – though strategically positioned rugs can be used as 'soft spots'.

Soft furnishings – the details

It is often the decorative details that will give the final flourish to a decorative scheme – the cushions, throws, lampshades, even tablecloths. Like an artist, you can put the final brushstrokes on your painting, placing colour, shape and emphasis with pinpoint accuracy. Equally, you might want to inject your room with very up-to-the-minute colours without spending a lot of money on upholstering a chair. To illustrate just how easily you can change the style of your room or the emphasis within it with mere details, just imagine a simple sofa, decorated with richly coloured, gold-tasselled velvet cushions and bolsters, and then the same sofa again, this time with crunchy linen cushions in neutral tones trimmed with natural rope braid.

Lampshades can be used to introduce interesting light effects; they work best in simple shapes and plain colours. In summer, when lamps may be purely ornamental during the day, their sculptural qualities must be considered, but in a winter room, where artificial light will play the dominant role, both lamp and lampshade are crucial to the creation of a welcoming atmosphere. If you do not want them to be translucent, look for lined shades: black will produce pools of light; pink tends to create a warm glowing ambience.

paint it, either finishing it with a protective coat of matt varnish, or using paints specially developed for floors. You could paint a border, or a quirky trompe-l'oeil pattern or focal point – either with a stencil or freehand.

Before going to the trouble of exposing and polishing a wooden floor, however, remember that you will have draughty ankles if the gaps between the floorboards are too large; acoustics might be a problem too if there are frequently to be a lot of people in the room at once. Rugs would help to minimize this echo, as well as providing texture, colour and pattern. Equally, you might use rugs of

SOFT FOCUS

The idea of using cream alone for the soft furnishings of a living room might at first seem bland and unexciting. By combining a variety of shades and textures within the same colour palette, however, you can achieve a surprising level of visual interest, whilst not distracting the eye from the intimate arrangement of the furniture – grouped wih conversation in mind. Cushions come in all manner of shapes and sizes, and soft feather cushions are particularly inviting. You can use them very self-consciously – either cumulatively or singly – to great effect.

Cream is not the ideal colour for a family with small children, but it is surprisingly robust. The various fabrics used here (opposite), from unbleached linen to delicate voile – one cover is even knitted – combine to create strong textural impact, while the dark parquet floor gives the cream tableau even greater definition.

Never underestimate the cost of good fabric nor the cost of reupholstering. A cheaper alternative is simply to cover a chair with a throw or quilt (left). Not only does this rejuvenate a tired chair, but it is a means of adding instant new colour, and life, to the room.

Window treatments

Whilst you should respond to the style and proportions of your room and the windows themselves, increasingly today windows seem characterized by clean-lined unfussiness.

Blinds are stylish, particularly if your room is small. Crisp and simple, well-fitting Roman blinds fold neatly into the window frame and can be lined for extra insulation. You can use a co-ordinating fabric if you are looking for another layer of pattern or colour. Venetian blinds, meanwhile, can be used to filter light during the day. Available in natural wood and an amazing range of colours, their hard-lined, stark appearance need no longer leave your room feeling bare and cold; instead your blinds can become an integral part of an overall colour scheme.

Slatted wooden shutters offer the same flexibility as regards shade, but are more expensive. As they are more solid, they might also 'feel' warmer than blinds; obviously, panelled shutters would be more effective. If privacy is a priority, or if you want to hide an unexciting view, half-height shutters are ideal. If you need a more delicate look, sheer cream or white blinds, an elegant modern alternative to net curtains, allow a soft, even light to pass through.

Softly falling curtains create an appropriately comfortable atmosphere; interlined, they are also ideal if you need to keep warmth in and draughts out. Remember that curtains should not obscure the window's features with overbearing details. An unfussy pelmet that will give the window a cleaner, more modern line is easily made of simple boards painted in a co-ordinating shade, and if you use plain fabrics and edge them boldy, you can give conventional curtains a contemporary twist. You can also combine blinds and curtains to dramatic effect.

Double glazing is now so accessible that insulation is less and less the primary function of a window treatment, though warmth and the illusion of warmth are still factors to consider. Privacy, easily overlooked, may also be high-priority status on your planning list.

Blinds are increasingly popular, as they do not intrude into the valuable room space as curtains and internal shutters once did, and they maximize any potential light. Venetian blinds (left above) are particularly flexible; not only do they give privacy without diminishing the light, they can be adjusted to alter the quality of light in the room. While metal blinds might seem severe, the modern wooden version is a gentler option, which seems to have acquired the timeless quality of a classic.

Curtain fabric can be quite expensive, but for a modest sum you can create elegant window treatments using plain fabric such as canvas, calico, or even muslin, and then drawing them up with decorative tie-backs (below left).

Warehouse apartment windows can be awkward to dress. Left almost bare (right), movable white panels can be raised or lowered to filter any harsh rays of blinding sunlight.

Display

Putting your favourite possessions on display is always a pleasurable job, but you must ensure that they suit the decorative style of the room, and are positioned against a background that sets them off to advantage. A well-loved collection is often the product of a lifetime's work, and consequently is always growing and changing; you will probably have to adjust your arrangements as time goes by in order to give your display enough space.

Make use of bookcases and shelves. It is a shame to allow these to be monopolized by serried ranks of books, however literary-minded you are, as they offer interesting

The unusually thick, purpose-built alcove shelves (opposite) have been designed specifically for the owner's collections of earthenware pots and basketware. The sheer simplicity of the pots – both in terms of colour and shape – sits very comfortably in this uncluttered, subtle room. One is tempted to ask whether the collection was bought as a whole to decorate the room, or whether the room was designed around an extant collection; more likely, the same person is probably responsible both for decorating the room and acquiring the collection, which explains why the combination is so sympathetic. A personal collection will always carry some aspect of its owner.

You can always give a favourite piece top billing by displaying it prominently on an easel or special stand (centre). A number of throws have been hung on a row of hooks on the adjacent wall: an easy and effective way of getting colour and pattern onto a wall – particularly if you need a temporary background.

An eclectic collection of objects (left), which combines nature and artifice, has a calm, uncluttered feel, despite the fact that the pictures have been included in the display instead of hanging above it.

display areas. You can be much more imaginative and create interesting still-lifes by combining on one shelf a few books, a vase and maybe a small ornament.

Generally speaking, people are becoming more daring about what they display on their walls. If, however, you do not feel entirely happy about being unconventional, you could put a completely diverse selection of pictures and photographs in identical frames and hang them in a self-consciously strong arrangement – three lines of three frames each, say – thereby lending a contemporary twist to apparently conventional formality.

It is probably best to restrict yourself to a few strong pieces in a minimalist interior, in order not to detract from the room's dramatic simplicity. They need not be large: the texture and formal qualities of a feather, shells, or even seaweed will be more than enough to create an impact.

STUDIOS

There is more to furnishing a studio room than using folding furniture. The multifunctional potential of the space has to be realized, bringing with it all the attendant problems that this entails – in magnified form. Niceties become necessities. When you do not have the luxury of dividing walls, and if you wish to create an attractive living space that both functions efficiently and offers you a peaceful sanctuary for those quiet, relaxing moments, disciplined early planning becomes even more vital.

DIVIDING SPACE

It might be helpful to study other small-scale living spaces – yacht cabins, beach huts, or garden pavilions, say – in order to glean elegant and functional design solutions that have evolved over some hundreds of years. With a ship's bunks in mind, therefore, you should take full advantage of a tall room: if you can construct a mezzanine gallery without being unsympathetic to your room's architectural proportions, you can give yourself another room – even if it is reached by ladder. The bedroom in this studio apartment (right) is in the eaves, above the cooking, eating and relaxing zones, a subtle low wall separating the functional kitchen and elegant dining area. Natural light from the rooflight is augmented by well-placed task lighting.

Screens and half-height walls can be used as temporary or more permanent dividers that do not reduce the flow of light. A Japanese-style opaque screen divides this room vertically (opposite) – beech-framed opaque glass replaces rice paper and bamboo. Screens are a good option in a studio because they not only allow you to differentiate between sleeping and living zones but also give you the chance to open up the space for larger-scale entertaining.

A living room that has to combine comfort with function is always a design challenge; in a studio's confined space the scale of that challenge is significantly increased. However, with meticulous planning you should be able to create a room that is both aesthetically pleasing and as multi-functional as you need it to be. Furnishing a small space no longer means having to sacrifice your design aspirations because, with space at a premium for everybody, there is an ever-increasing range of options available.

Your personal life will have to be on show to the public in a studio more than in any other domestic situation. Today, however, creating a tranquil sanctuary where you can unwind is just as – if not more – important, particularly if you live amidst urban noise and pressures. So, before you immerse yourself in colour charts and furniture brochures, sit down and ask yourself whether you want to fill your life with people or whether you will keep this as your own private haven, going out when you feel sociable.

If the latter, put the emphasis on comfort, and give yourself easy access to your favourite books and music, and the television too, perhaps. Look at how high a priority sleep is in your essentials list: do you want your bed to feel like a permanent fixture, or are you happy to transform your world every morning and evening from bedroom to living room and back again? This decision may be coloured by whether you will be working at home, for to be able to work effectively, you will need to create a less relaxed atmosphere. Do not forget to consider mundane issues like laundry: heaps of washing and regular trips to laundromats can become very stressful, so you may decide that finding a space for a washing machine is essential, however unprepossessing it might be in aesthetic terms. You should

BEIGE IS COOL

You should decide, when you make your floor plan, where you will position all your furniture, considering any electrical or plumbing needs at the same time. Organized at the start, lighting can be arranged to emphasize different parts of the room at different times, creating the feeling of more space.

The owner of this tiny square living space has created an interesting space out of a regularly shaped room by blocking off one corner with a wooden-cladded partition. This 'screen' is thick enough to display large pots and boxes on the top; hidden behind it is a desk.

Light floods in through the windows, the pale colour scheme enhancing the airy feeling. Appropriately, the room has been devoted to day-time living. At night the arms of the sofa are lowered and a double bed is revealed. If you buy a sofabed, it really is worth opting for an expensive one with a fully sprung mattress. Whilst a cheap sofabed might suffice for the occasional overnight stay, it will not be sturdy enough for daily use.

Storage consists of one mobile floor-to-ceiling unit of cube-shaped lockers, holding everything from magazines to kitchen equipment, and a tall painted chest of drawers for clothes.

think about storage, lighting and heating at planning stage, too. These are all crucial issues in the design equation, when you come to focus on which functions are to be given what emphasis in your limited space.

You may have a room large enough to allow you to create zones, giving each function a certain permanence. Generally, however, you are unlikely to have enough square footage to furnish so expansively; instead you will probably have to utilize every inch of space in a considered way if you wish to avoid a haphazard jumble of furniture.

Chaotic arrangements take up valuable floor space; and even the most ingenious space-saving furniture cannot save you from the resulting irritations. If you position all the furniture around the perimeter of the room, however, you will leave yourself a useful space in the middle, without forfeiting any sense of cosiness – whereas a larger room furnished like this might look like a waiting room.

It will still be crucial to have hardworking furniture to realize your perfect design, and today furniture-makers are increasingly combining space-saving features with stylish design. There are folding chairs, for instance, to suit the full spectrum of decorative styles; tables, traditional or contemporary, that expand and contract to suit your needs – either by inserting leaves or with gate-legged 'wings' that can be folded up or down, independently or in pairs. There is no point in having a table that can expand, however, if you have not provided enough room to open it.

The same goes for a sofabed, which tends to be the first essential furniture requirement for one-room living. It is no fun having to shift coffee tables and armchairs every night before you can unfold the bed. The classic day bed offers an interesting alternative. Even the simplest can be

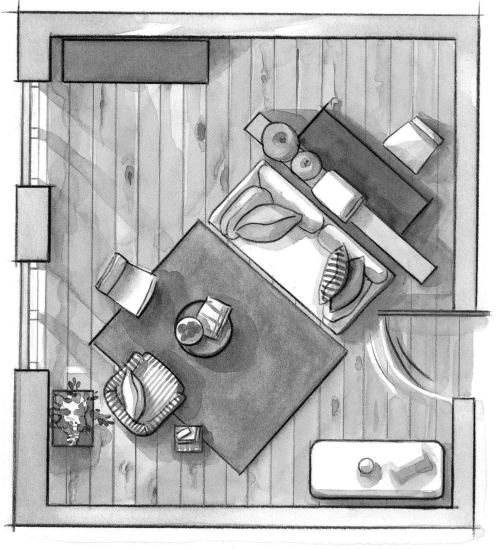

You can never over-estimate your storage needs because even if you do not use the space immediately, you soon will. Moreover, in a studio good storage is essential for your own sanity. So it is even more crucial that you choose storage units that either perform more than one function or are craftily designed to accommodate different objects. Decide what you would like to keep on show and what is better behind doors or in boxes and then you should be able to find storage that sits well with your decorative style.

A metal trunk (opposite) is efficiently multifunctional. It is capacious enough to hold filing and oddly shaped items; would make an attractive coffee table; and, as it is on wheels, is easily moved out of the way, or to wherever it is most useful.

Consider investing in a state-of-the-art hi-fi system – if only for its tiny dimensions. Purpose-built panelled cupboards (far left) can house a huge collection of CDs. Taking up minimal space, they are here built to dado height so the top also provides a useful platform for the appropriately tiny music system itself and for display.

A wall of floor-to-ceiling built-in units can combine hidden storage and open shelves As nothing protrudes into the body of the room, and aided by reflective metal doors, it appears to take up minimal space.

dressed up during the day, almost to suit your mood. Swathed in natural calico, bright silks or even wild animal prints, it can also be a strong focal point in a studio room.

This is not the moment for impulse purchases; take the floor plan and measurements when you go to buy furniture because a vast showroom will distort the dimensions and proportions of any piece and it is costly to discover that the sofa that looked so compact in the shop in fact dwarfs everything in the living room – you may have a struggle even to get it through the door. If you choose furniture that appears to take up less room than it actually does – wicker, for example – you will make your space feel bigger, and creating a sense of space is every bit as important as space itself. Strategically placed mirrors and glass can help, too.

Loose covers allow for easy and frequent cleaning – essential if you wish to retain a constantly fresh look; two sets will allow you to vary the atmosphere of the room – seasonally perhaps. Similarly, you may like curtains for warmth in the winter but prefer to undress your windows for a more spacious, fine-lined look during the hotter, brighter months – but this requires more storage capacity.

Avoid complicated decorating schemes. It is probably best to restrict your palette; it is much easier to display a disparate selection of pictures on a plain ground than on a pattern. A pale shade will give a feeling of light and space.

Simplicity is the key. Keep everything clean and easy on the eye and you will create a relaxed space that adapts easily from function to function.

INDEX

Page numbers in italic refer
to the illustrations

PUBLISHERS' ACKNOWLEDGMENTS

The Publishers would like to thank the following photographers and organizations for their kind permission to reproduce the photographs in this book:

1 David Montgomery/House and Garden/Condé Nast Publications; 2 Sanderson Design Archive; 2 Dennis Brandsma/VT Wonen; 3 Otto Polman/Ariadne; 4–5 Dennis Brandsma/VT Wonen; 6–7 Paul Warchol (Architect: Phillip Teft); 8–9 James Merrell/The World of Interiors; 9 right Alexander van Berge/VT Wonen; 10 Marie-Pierre Morel/Marie Kalt/Marie Claire Maison; 11 Ray Main (Circus Architects); 12 Paul Ryan/International Interiors (Designers: Gordon/De Vries); 13 Ted Yarwood (Designer: Sharon Mimran); 14 Hotze Eisma/Ariadne; 15 Hans Zeegers/VT Wonen; 16 below Peter Aprahamian (Architect: Nico Rench); 16 above Alexander van Berge/VT Wonen; 17 Cecilia Innes/The Interior Archive; 18 Nicholas Tosi/Julie Borgeaud/Marie Claire Maison; 19 Verne Fotografie (Architect: Antonio Citerio, Milan); 20–21 Marston & Langinger Limited, 192 Ebury Street, London; 22 Marie-Pierre Morel/Daniel Rozensztroch (Architect: Paula Navone); 23 Earl Carter/Vogue Living; 24–25 Fritz von der Schulenburg/The Interior Archive (Designers: Adelheid von der Schulenburg and John Stefanidis); 26–27 Simon Kenny/Belle Magazine (Architect: Utz-Sanby); 28–29 Dennis Brandsma/VT Wonen; 29 right David Phelps; 30 Fritz von der Schulenburg/The Interior Archive (Designer: John Stefanidis); 31 Paul Ryan/International Interiors (Designers: Chuck and Martha Baker); 32 Fritz von der Schulenburg/The Interior Archive (Designer: Dot Spikings); 33 above left Fritz von der Schulenburg/The Interior Archive (Designer: Dot Spikings); 33 above right Maura McEvoy; 33 below Paul Ryan/International Interiors (Designer: Kristiina Ratia); 34 Alexander van Berge/VT Wonen; 35 left Paul Ryan/International Interiors (Designer: Christian Liaigre); 35 right Paul Warchol (Architects: Pei Partnership); 36 above Alan Weintraub/Arcaid; 36 below Lu Jeffery (Rachel Cooke); 37 Ray Main; 38 above Hans Zeegers/VT Wonen; 38 below Ted Yarwood (Designers: Michelle Lloyd/David Berman); 38–39 Hans Zeegers/VT Wonen; 40–41 Ted Yarwood (Designers: Michelle Lloyd and David Berman); 41 right Jonathan Pilkington/Homes and Gardens/Robert Harding Syndication; 42 Paul Ryan/International Interiors (Designers: Casdin/John Saladino); 43 Spike Powell/Abode; 44–45 Jurgen Frank/J.B. Visual Press (Ellen O'Neill's house); 45 right Pia Tryde/ Homes and Gardens/Robert Harding Syndication; 46–47 Marie–Pierre Morel/Christine Puech/Marie Claire Maison; 48 Tim Beddow/Interior Archive (Architect: Craig Hamilton); 49 Marie-Pierre Morel/Daniel Rozensztroch/Marie Claire Maison; 50 Richard Davies/Elle Decoration; 51 Hotze Eisma; 52–53 Hotze Eisma/Ariadne; 53 Penelope Chauvelot/M. Bocquillom/Marie France; 54 Pia Tryde/Homes and Garden/Robert Harding Syndication; 55 above Jeff Lung/Vogue Living (Architect: Glenn Murcutt for Judy and Ken Done); 55 below Dennis Brandsma/VT Wonen; 56 below Paul Ryan/International Interiors (Designer: Francis Halliday); 56 above Verne Fotografie; 57 James Merrell/The World of Interiors (Designer: Jonathan Reed); 58–59 William Waldron/Courtesy of House Beautiful (Designers: Mallory/James); 59 right Andrew Cameron/Country Homes and Interiors/Robert Harding Syndication; 61 Jerome Darblay; 62 above left Fritz von der Schulenburg/The Interior Archive (Designer: John Stefanidis); 62 above right Nadia Mackenzie; 62 below Dennis Brandsma/VT Wonen; 63 above right Verne Fotografie (Designer: Vicente Wolf, NY); 64 Gilles de Chabaneix/Marie Kalt/Marie Claire Maison; 65 Hotze Eisma/Ariadne; 66 above Andreas von Einsiedel (Reed/Boyd Design); 66 below J.F.Jaussaud/Inside (Designer F. Mechiche); 67 Paul Ryan/International Interiors (Designers: Kathy Moskal/Ken Foreman); 68 left Christoph Kicherer (Architect: Tony Doherty/Designer: Stephen Falckes, South Africa); 68 right Ted Yarwood (Designers: Michelle Lloyd and David Berman); 69 Verne Fotografie (Designer: Vicente Wolf, NY); 70–71 Nicolas Tosi/Catherine Ardouin/Marie Claire Maison; 71 right Dennis Brandsma/VT Wonen; 72 Jeff Hay/Vogue Living; 73 Ken Hayden (Designer: Jonathan Reed); 74–75 Neues Wohnen/Camera Press; 76 Alexander van Berge/VT Wonen; 77 Dennis Brandsma/VT Wonen

AUTHOR'S ACKNOWLEDGMENTS

I would like to say a huge thank you to Joanna Laidlaw for her friendship and inspiration; to Emma Warlow for spending a helpful day with me; to my children who could not believe anyone could take so long to write a book; and at Conran Octopus to Sarah Sears, my editor, who deserves a medal, and also to Amanda Lerwill and Helen Fickling.